W9-BVM-444

LAUGHING
DOWN
LONELY
CANYONS

OTHER BOOKS BY JAMES KAVANAUGH

NON-FICTION

There's Two Of You
Man In Search of God
Journal of Renewal
A Modern Priest Looks At His Outdated Church
The Struggle Of the Unbeliever (Limited Edition)
The Birth of God
Between Man and Woman (co-authored)
Search: A Guide For Those Who Dare Ask Of
Life Everything Good and Beautiful

POETRY

There Are Men Too Gentle To Live Among Wolves
Will You Be My Friend?
Faces In The City
America: A Ballad
The Crooked Angel (children's book)
Sunshine Days and Foggy Nights
Maybe If I Loved You More
Winter Has Lasted Too Long
Walk Easy On the Earth
Laughing Down Lonely Canyons
Today I Wondered About Love
(Adaptation of: Will You Still Love Me?)
From Loneliness To Love
Tears and Laughter Of A Man's Soul

FICTION:

A Coward For Them All
The Celibates

ALLEGORY:

Celebrate the Sun: A Love Story
A Village Called Harmony—A Fable

LAUGHING
DOWN
LONELY
CANYONS

James Kavanaugh

Illustrations by Heather Preston

 Steven J. Nash Publishing
Highland Park, Illinois
1-800-843-8545

LAUGHING DOWN LONELY CANYONS

Laughing Down Lonely Canyons. Copyright © 1984 by James Kavanaugh. Illustrations copyright © 1984 by Heather preston. All rights reserved. Printed in the U.S.A. No part of this book may be used without written permission except for brief quotes. Write: Steven J. Nash Publishing, P.O. Box 2115, Highland Park, IL 60035.

8 editions published by Harper and Row, San Francisco. Designed by Donna Davis.

Library of Congress Catalogue #90-062965

Kavanaugh, James J.
    Laughing down lonely canyons
    I. Title

      ISBN # 1-878995-11-1   First Steven J. Nash Edition
                            Copyright ©1990 by James Kavanaugh

Ninth printing

20   19   18   17   16   15   14   13   12   11   10   9

INTRODUCTION

Gradually I have learned to believe that life is more than mere existence, that there is a subtle plan for each of us according to our individual gifts and private yearnings. There is a quiet inner rhythm guiding us once we decide to live as individuals and not remain paralyzed by the persistent threat of abandonment carried from childhood. We can cease hiding or running, face fears and persistent anxieties, and create a realistic, genuine dream no matter how long it takes. To become whole as we are destined to be, to let go and roll laughing down lonely canyons.

Often we abandon our dream and surrender to what seems inevitable because we have lived with childhood fantasies too grandiose ever to be realized. Ultimately we endure a marriage grown silent, work at a job we can barely tolerate, and ignore our personal feelings until we no longer really know what we want. To survive, we retreat into a prison of our own making. We exist, perform, even achieve an unsatisfying success, dismissing yearnings for intimacy and change as distant impossibilities. We accept life as a burden to be endured with no time to let go and run laughing down lonely canyons.

This is not to say that we never know happiness, but that life remains a competitive struggle and does not deliver what it seemed to promise. There were so many youthful hopes and exciting options, but somehow enthusiasm dries up and a vague loneliness or quiet depression lurks in frightened eyes or drawn faces as a constant companion. Life becomes security and survival, a painful struggle that prays for miraculous release, and a child's spontaneity is denied adults who fear to let go and skip laughing down lonely canyons.

We close our eyes and ears to shut out pain, numb our senses to endure the tedious day and unfriendly night, and cling to whatever or whomever is at hand to save us. We work harder, read more, turn to magic or illusion, sex or power or money. We no longer turn to ourselves or to others where real strength and love are possible. Fear and apparent failure have overwhelmed us. But we are stronger than we know, more resilient and courageous, more loving and lovable than we think. And it is personal courage and active love that will free us to roll laughing down lonely canyons.

This is a book for the barely brave and beginning lovers like me, who refuse to abandon their dream, now more humble and real, and struggle to meet life and even death head on. It is for those who value personal freedom as their most precious gift and want to make of life the joy it was meant to be. It is for those who refuse to give up no matter the pain, who know the worth of intimate love and friendship, and who recognize the power of God, by whatever name, that lives within us. It is a book for those who, despite all, will continue to let go and run forever laughing down lonely canyons.

JAMES KAVANAUGH
Reno, Nevada

LAUGHING
DOWN
LONELY
CANYONS

To those who have crawled inch by inch
from greyness to light;

To those who have climbed a mountain
despite fear and darkness;

To those who know that laughter
is the greatest gift of the gods.

and gratefully
To those who have laughed with me
down lonely canyons.

Laughing Down Lonely Canyons

Fear corrodes my dreams tonight and mist has greyed
    my hills,
Mountains seem too tall to climb, December winds
    are chill.
There's no comfort on the earth, I am a child
    abandoned,
    Till I feel your hand in mine
    And laugh down lonely canyons.

Snow has bent the trees in grief, my summer dreams
    are dead,
Flowers are but ghostly stalks, the clouds drift
    dull as lead.
There's no solace in the sky, I am a child abandoned,
    Till we chase the dancing moon
    And laugh down lonely canyons.

Birds have all gone south too soon and frogs refuse to
    sing,
Deer lie hidden in the woods, the trout asleep till
    spring.
There's no wisdom in the wind, I am a child
    abandoned,
    Till we race across the fields
    And laugh down lonely canyons.

Darkness comes too soon tonight, the trees are silent
    scars,
Rivers rage against the rocks and snow conceals the
    stars.
There's no music in the air, I am a child abandoned,
    Till I feel my hand in yours
    And laugh down lonely canyons.

The Sun Lingers

The sun lingers over the ocean a little longer tonight,
While I remember everyone I love
    And wish I could hold them in my arms all at
      once.
Words are so futile to speak of love, to heal hurts so
    pointless and unintended.
Perhaps life's greatest pain and longing is the
    loneliness of missing friends I cannot call to my
    side.
Curse time and distance and all the banalities of life
    that tear us apart.
I didn't know when I left home I would leave the
    brothers I loved.
Time was so omnipresent, we had every day, every
    meal, forever.
I wish as I watch the disappearing sun that I could
    gather together all those I love and all that love
    me,
And remain in one house, one town, one union.
No one left out, no one unavailable, no one whose
    voice and words and smile could not be at my
    beck and call.
I miss you all so much,
    And love you all so profoundly,
And refuse to understand a world and destiny that
    keeps us apart.
But I am grateful for the friends that life has
    permitted to remain,

Grateful for the memories, the reunions that lie
ahead,
The laughs and tears and stories that cannot be
told enough,
Grateful that the sun lingers over the ocean a little
longer tonight.

I Want to Walk with You
Above the Pines

I want to walk with you above the pines,
> *Scale mountains, leap rivers, speak to the sun
> and moon,*
And make wagers with the stars.
I want to roll laughing down lonely canyons,
> *To tease the desert that threatens to destroy, ski
> deserted trails,*
*Ride dirt bikes to the very edge of the lingering
horizon.*
*I want to sail across strange seas and explore buried
cities,*
> *To watch the mating of whales in a Mexican
> lagoon,*
*And hear the music of coyotes resound across a
moonless sky.*
*I want to startle deer in forests and mountain lions in
their lairs,*
> *To surprise bold raccoons and watch the porcupines
> waddle away*
Like embarrassed little boys.
But most of all I want to love without barriers,
> *With eyes laughing and hearts singing
> And caution abandoned to the clouds by a
> friendly west wind.*
*I want to feel your presence as my very own, to speak
to you as though*
*I am talking to myself, to hold you without fear or
distance
Or private thoughts.*

So I can walk with you above the pines, scale
mountains, leap rivers,
Speak to the sun and moon
And make wagers with the stars.

I Need to Know

I need to know I am loved
Far beyond coffee in the morning and a favorite
meal.
I need eyes looking at me as if there is no other left on
earth
Words to tell me why I have been chosen from all
the rest.
I need caresses, love notes, an arm locked in mine,
Fingers on my face, hands brushing back my
hair.
I am strong only in my capacity to endure pain,
In my determination not to be overwhelmed by
shadows that appear without permission
and endure without reason.
I am strong in confronting the fears that match each
decade of my life,
In not looking back with guilt and regrets,
In my persistent reassurance that all my dreams
will be realized.
I am strong when it is essential to someone that I live,
Unthinkable that I die, unbearable that I
disappear,
A love that goes all out without reservation or
calculation,
A love of total trust and total loyalty,
A love that can last until I breathe my last breath and
gaze my last gaze—at you,
When I am finally glad that I have lived
Because I know how much I have been loved.

In Celebration of You!

I have tried to imagine my world without you:
    Soaring geese in formation, mountain peaks
        hidden in snow,
    The splendor of fall along a country road,
    The whirr of a ring-necked pheasant at midday,
    The bleating of a horned owl at midnight,
And know that none of it would be the same
    Without you.
But most of all,
    I could never replace your smile, your eyes,
    Your gentleness and giving, your loyalty and
        caring,
    The memories we've filed, the secrets we've
        shared.
    The love that is forever there despite time or
        distance.
So, today I celebrate your very existence,
    Thank all of life for your life,
    Express my deepest gratitude that
        Of the millions of people and possibilities,
        Our lives were destined to be intermingled.
And as I celebrate your being,
    I want you to know, clearly and forever,
    That my world would never be the same,
Without you.

Mad Distortions of Reality

Mad distortions of reality,
Jealousy destroying trusting love,
Crippled fantasies piled on crippled fantasies,
More powerful than any words.
Who will relieve the sordid thoughts that tear my
        soul apart,
        That leave me exhausted and angry and
                stretched inside-out
        Like some broken rubber doll?
Who will restore balance and sanity when
        suspicion seems like fact
        And insecurity creates its own miasmic world?
Do you not understand that love endures beyond
        the horrors of troubled moments, that
        freedom is the path of love and the child must
        finally give up searching for his mother?
Your mind will destroy you with its mad assumptions,
        As if what is yours can be taken away by any
                peddler selling his wares.
Retreat within your soul, sing melodies to what is,
        The stars, the moon, the days and nights together.
There are millions of hungry men and women
        begging for attention,
        Looking for a soothing word or refreshing hand.
Only the strong and trusting can venture out—the
        rest must linger in the shadows—begging that
        every least alms be theirs.

A Friendship Like Ours

A friendship like ours is without pretence or barriers,
Where no word is without consequence, no pain
without compassion,
When time means nothing and distance is as
insignificant as astral travel,
Where a single word can sometimes say all there is to
say,
And love grows organically each passing day,
Where misunderstandings are impossible and words
have no currency,
Where a chance meeting is enough to last a lifetime,
And heart speaks to heart in a single contact.
I have known good and gentle men and women for a
lifetime,
Have been bound to them by blood and debt and
every circumstance,
Even lashed together by work and space and
passionate concern,
Yet few of these could invade the privacy of my inner
being
No matter their power or brilliance, beauty or
wealth.
But you were destined to reside there, my friend by
an eternal edict,
Because even before we met,
You were already there!

There Are Days

There are days when I miss your slow smile and
    kittens
        Crawling through a broken window in the
            morning.
Your earth tones and wind-blown taste, your stretch
    marks
        Like a wise and wrinkled face,
Your lips, soft, devouring waves, your eyes attending
    all I say
        Like shining beacons, absorbed and inseparable.
We could not kiss or touch or devour enough,
        Like peanut butter and jelly and warm bread
            dripping with butter
Your breasts flowing from your body
        Like grass hills, warm and languorous in the
            sunshine,
Your nipples like chocolate stars of childhood,
        Sweet and lingering with a voice all their own.
Your helpless clucks and sighs of passion,
        Your eyes clenched with pain and pleasure in
            sweet conflict.
So much in love, so riveted and freeing all at once,
        Asking little and giving more than I could ever
            want.
It did not matter where or what,
        Weeping at Carmelite nuns
            Chanting their vesper song,
        Weeping from instinctive innocence at too much
            beauty.

11

Laughing over margaritas and loving in the
parking lot,
Laughing on the beach, grinding our backs
And scarring our legs in wet sand at midnight,
Rolling crazily like children and finally
adults.
Even now I often long for you in quiet reverie
And know that in another's bed
You still remember the snow, the mountains,
The new coats at Christmas,
Poems you cried about or laughed about
until you cried.
Now your voice is only silent to prevent pain and
impossibilities.
Love has its time and place, its moments and
destiny,
Love is an option that's lost if not exercised.
But, at times, it seems strange
That such madness and passion as ours
Are only the memories of some forgotten
day,
And I am left with the trace of a slow, warm smile,
And kittens crawling through a broken window
in the morning.

So Often

So often I stand like a bashful child,
   Speechless before those I love,
Wanting to tell them all that is in my heart,
But frightened by some distance in their eyes.
Thus, so much of life is lived all alone,
   So many conversations with one's self go
      unanswered.
I would like to begin again, do it all right this time.
   There would be no docile, frightened adolescent,
      Smiling endlessly to hide his anger
      Trampling on his own fears
      Ignoring his private dreams
      Fighting for some recognition that never
         came from within.
No one could push or prod me,
No one could intimidate or smother me,
No one could drive me to adore a God
   I didn't understand.
Strange! Even as a little boy I knew it was all wrong,
   That life was far more than docility and duty
      and self-annihilation!
All these years spent reclaiming that child who was
   instinctively wiser than all his teachers,
All these years spent trying to recapture what I
   surrendered to frightened preachers,
Until I can only ask that the loving, prodigal child
   who was lost will finally reappear,
So that life is the circle it was meant to be,
   That the child who flowered at life's beginning
   Will once more flourish at its end.

Want Ad

Mature Man: badly bruised by life,
Abandoned by two wives and three lovers,
Father of three grown children who consider him
*   eccentric but nice.*
Has good job and adequate income and savings
And seeks suitable mate of any reasonable age.
Requests devotion and meals, caring and love at
*   regular or irregular intervals.*
Dislikes arguments, punk rock, Fantasy Island, and
*   canned spaghetti.*
Friendly, can be very funny, skis, plays tennis, will
*   dance upon prolonged teasing.*
Has friends, likes to travel, read, converse, and
*   explore deserted beaches.*
Dreams are presently dulled by unexplained midlife
*   sadness.*
Needs more than pills and therapy to recapture
*   confidence and joy of living.*
Sexually very well disciplined, somewhat emotionally
*   repressed, capable of long periods of silence.*
Eager to grow, live, love, and be a lifelong friend.
Can fix garbage disposal, faulty toilet, clogged drains.
Hates yard work and laundry, but does do windows.
References available upon request: one from a golden
*   retriever, another from a siamese cat.*
Average size, decent looks, adequate personality.
Send name, number, and picture to Box 89.

Marlene

Marlene's depression is only the stored-up passion
   That accepted a Mercedes and a house on the
      hill
   For the madness of a love her whole body
      screamed for.
Had she never tasted love like an alien at a cheese
   and sausage store,
Had she never smelled its pungence an inch from her
   face
   Fearing its power as much as she hungered for it,
She would be as grateful as all her neighbors
   Whose very inflection is as predictable as a
      keyboard.
But she had a vision, however brief, of what love
   could be,
   One of the few, perhaps,
   One of the blessed or cursed, perhaps,
And she traded it away for credit cards and no more
   studying prices at the Safeway store.
Now she has it all. Save a great love.
Even children are not enough.
Her whole being rises up cyclically like the earth
   With the rage of recurring depression,
   To which pills bring brief respite,
But only love or death brings release.

Henry

Henry's the only guy I know who never graduated
from childhood,
Even though he has his own business
And has as much trouble with the IRS and
government regulations as anyone else.
It's just that work is only a game with Henry
And he can stop and talk in the midst of a major
deal
As if he were still shooting marbles in the
playground.
If you met him at lunch, you wouldn't know if he
taught kindergarten,
Played a saxophone, or was rebuilding an old
T-Bird.
You wouldn't know if he were rich or poor, a bank
clerk or its president,
A weekend refugee from a funny farm or a
successful inventor of video games.
He's curious about everything from hang gliders to
daffodils,
Wonders about sourdough bread and the
difference between good kings and bad
presidents.
He likes books, movies, music, baseball, orchids,
pelicans, cars,
Tennis, trout fishing, parrots, prostitutes, and
antiques.
He is fascinated with dinosaurs, bats, God, turtles,
sailboats,
Swans, nuns, bridge, crossword puzzles, and
scuba diving.

I don't know anyone he doesn't like, any food he
doesn't eat,
Any game he doesn't play, any animal he doesn't
love.
He laughs at everything, especially at himself, cries
at funerals
And sad movies, and remembers birthdays like
an insurance man.
He celebrates weddings, births, sunny days, rainy
afternoons,
The first robin, the last goose, victories, defeats,
and rainbows.
And is the only guy I know who never graduated
from childhood.

Purvis

Purvis was a firm sort of man
    When he married Doxie,
Sure of himself, quick to decide, strict with the kids,
    The kind of man you wouldn't push too far,
    Quiet until there was a good reason to be loud,
Then he bellowed until he could be heard two blocks
    away—
Followed by very good sex.
After ten years of marriage, Purvis changed,
    Caught in a job-loss and a feminist crossfire
    When Doxie joined a woman's group that taught
        her to be
    Assertive, aggressive, and stingy with sex.
Purvis sought psychiatric help and soon became
    As gentle, soft, tolerant, and understanding as
        his analyst.
He stopped bellowing—followed by very mediocre sex.
Doxie told him assertively what a weakling he was,
    aggressively
    Got a good job as an office manager,
    And complained that Purvis had lost his spunk.
A month ago she left him for a salesman,
    The firm kind of man you wouldn't push too far,
    Quiet until there was a reason to be loud,
Then he bellowed until he could be heard two blocks
    away—
Followed by very good sex.

Harold

Harold is a visitor from another planet
Where words have a dozen meanings
And God is a friend Who rides on his motorcycle.
He laughs louder than earthlings, certainly more
often,
Talks in circles and squares and geometric
patterns yet to be discovered.
He's had a hundred jobs and lost most of them
Because nobody knew what he was talking about
or laughing at.
He's wise if you can follow his winding words,
Gentle if you take the time to listen,
Loving if you comprehend what he's
laughing at.
So many deceitful people speak in cautious logic,
While Harold, beyond deceit, beyond definition,
beyond description,
Speaks in parallelograms and laughs in eight-sided
triangles.
A thousand people gave up on him, parents, friends,
Eminent doctors who scratched their heads and
admitted he was from a different universe.
Fortunately Harold gives up on no one, especially
Harold,
Content to follow not merely a "distant drummer,"
But a whole distant galaxy
Of geometric patterns and love words—yet to be
discovered.

Herman

Herman's older now and well off
  By any standards but his own,
    Wondering if inflation will dissolve his
      savings,
    Wondering if property tax will steal his
      home,
    Wondering if the banks will fail like they
      did before.
He's got municipal bonds and real estate, social
    security, stocks,
    And a couple of sound investments in
      apartment houses.
But Herman wonders what happens if the tenants
    can't pay or move out,
    If the stocks go down, the bonds disintegrate, and
      social security goes belly up.
So every night he adds up what he's got,
    Divides it by the rate of inflation
    And how long he's got to live,
    Computes it all carefully enough
      To know that he won't be wiped out
        tomorrow.
Only then does he smile, sip a bourbon, play
    backgammon with his wife,
    And sleeps like a baby—until the morning—
When he starts wondering again
    What'll happen if he lives to be ninety like his
      Uncle Al.

One of Those Years

It's been one of those years of colds and strange
infections
When immortality gets shaky and I wish poets could
afford insurance that covers more than terminal
something.
So I decided to start listening to the half of California
that makes a living giving holistic health tips to
the other half.
I began by drinking two gallons of water a day as
advised to flush out all the poisons
Until I learned at a wedding reception that I was
abusing my kidneys and absorbing aquatic
impurities.
So I turned to milk at the suggestion of a bearded
nutritionist with puffy cheeks
Until I heard that all "dairy" was dangerous after
infancy and cheese giveaways were related to
genocide.
Later a lean ascetic insisted that citrus fruits were
suitable only for people in the tropics,
And since the experts said I wasn't far north enough
for red meat, nor far south enough for dedicated
vegetarianism,
I either had to move to Alaska or rely on vitamins.
When I chose vitamins out of deference to high
interest rates, an oriental homeopath insisted I
needed minerals.
Everyone agreed that green vegetables were
outstanding except a Stanford nutritionist who
said they caused depression
And truly sensible digestions included cereals, brown
rice, and four aspirin a day.

*An eminent doctor with two books once in print said
    to listen to my body,*
*But when my body requested two dozen chocolate
    chip cookies and a quart of rocky road ice
    cream, he sighed and said I was starved for
    protein.*
*So without water, oranges, red meat, green
    vegetables, or chocolate chip cookies,*
*I've been living on Jack Daniels and fritos and
    haven't felt better for months.*

Him and Her

Him: *Where do you wanna eat tonight?*
Her: *I don't know what I feel like—*
Giovanni's is always good, and Jose's—or the
cute little French place Myrtle is always raving
about.
Him: *I'm just hungry. It's only one meal.*
We don't have to make a federal case out of it.
Her: *Does a nice filet sound good? You always like*
filet. With a nice baked potato and roquefort
salad. Are you real hungry or just kind of
hungry?
Him: *I'm losing my appetite.*
Her: *That natural food place has nice omelettes. Do*
you feel like an omelette or something heavier?
Him: *I'm beginning to feel terrible!*
Her: *Maybe we ought to pick up a few pork chops. You*
probably want to eat at home.
Him: *I don't care where we eat. Let's just eat!*
Her: *Okay! It's done! What do you feel like?*

Apartment Hunting Again

Apartment hunting again,
Scanning the papers for the perfect spot
>*To write poetry and make coffee in the*
>>*morning,*
>*To listen to music and drink wine in the*
>>*afternoon,*
>*To follow the moon and make love in the*
>>*evening.*
It's easy now to interpret the ad-code after a half
>*dozen years*
>*And a dozen moves:*
"One bedroom guest house, unusual" means a moldy
>*garage shared with a boa constrictor.*
"Rustic" means filthy and probably without plumbing,
"Unusual view" means a neighbor's fence and
>*doughboy pool and a glimpse of the mountains*
>*from the top of the garage.*
"Country kitchen" means warped drawers, no
>*garbage disposal, and roaches playing tag in the*
>*sink.*
"Secluded" means there are no street lights and
>*you're a mile and a half from the Seven-Eleven.*
"Artist's dream" means a decayed arbor with ivy and
>*spiders covering all the windows.*
"Recently remodeled" means linoleum, beige carpets,
>*and green walls.*
"Pets and children okay" means the building's in
>*foreclosure.*
"A doll house" means you can't open the bathroom
>*door without knocking over the kitchen table,*

And "quaint" means the landlord buys his furniture
    at yard sales.
When you finally decide that, with first and last
    month's rent and a security deposit, you're better
    off making a down-payment on your own place,
    please be advised that a "handyman's dream"
    means
You shouldn't enter the area without a shotgun.

Death Valley Revisited

*Hundreds of trailers and campers of every size and
     condition gather in the winter in Death Valley,
Distant kinfolk of covered wagons and eager forty-
     niners.
Thousands of tired, gentle eyes gazing patiently at the
     silent desert
          With time to watch the sun disappear too
               suddenly behind mountain peaks and leave
               them cold and lonesome.
Faces no longer fighting time or wrinkles or the
     madness of survival,
Finally content to be overweight and underachieved,
     to gather their souvenir borax in a gift shop.
No longer twenty healthy mules in the whole valley,
     only the scattered burros, friendly, fuzzy relics
     of overworked forebears,
Not unlike the retired trailer people—"Marv and
     Dixie"—"Ed and Hazel Jones"—immortalized
     on the backs of Air Streams and Open Roads,
Ready like children to laugh at anything, finally even
     themselves,
Crowded together in narrow watering holes and
     huddled around campfires for sing-a-longs and
     Duke and Ellie's chili,
Finally unafraid of Indians or avalanche, boiling air
     or starvation,
Only privately fearing emptiness and death and
     crippling illness,
Grinning at ready-made friends and hootenanny
     entertainment and telling too many stories
     about their grandkids.*

The children are gone now, scattered to their own
    success or misfortune, unaware that Death
    Valley and trailers will arrive.
When men and women settle for the love and
    tenderness they have, knowing well that nothing
    half as comfortable lies ahead.
No more greedy demands on life, no new tragedy that
    has not been met and endured. Only death
    remains.
The crossing of some unfamiliar but not unfriendly
    gulch they stare at in the twilight while coyotes
    moan like waiting angels.
The end seems only as far away as ghostly Indians
    hiding in the hills, as distant as nameless
    mountain peaks whose profiles have not changed
    for centuries.
"Ain't that Ed a kick with his big Mexican hat!"—
    "And Artie knows a thousand jokes that wheeze
    you into a sideache."
The rows of grey clouds settle over the campers like
    ancient tribes lined up for judgment, the sands
    shift restlessly over buried wagons or buckboards,
    withered wine casks or bleached skeletons,
Then buries them again and again as silent
    reminders of life and death and the whispering
    echoes of Death Valley.
Maybe the Indians will pour down from the hills,
    riding their ponies and brandishing their bows,
    to bring new light to the eyes
That stare wistfully off into the desert distance, or
    gather to play the canasta games that only end
    with death.
Then Ed puts on his Mexican hat and Artie tells his
    jokes until the moon rises and eyes grow dim as
    the campfires.

*Marv and Dixie settle into each other's arms, so do Ed
and Hazel Jones, and the trailers are as silent as
the desert, and the love as pure and lasting as
any on the earth.*
*Then morning will come, and coffee, memories and
the subtle life of the desert, as gentle and fragile
and mysterious as their own.*

Once Your Eyes

Once your eyes rested on me like a child, helpless to
*   look away.*
Now they drift into shadows or beg to be amused like
*   a restless puppy.*
Is security the ultimate oath that love will never be?
Is contrived gentleness the only currency in
*   circulation?*
I like raging men, unreasonable men, outrageous
*   men*
*   Who know a love the feeble and frightened never*
*   understand.*
I am no manservant, no prisoner chained by
*   contracts,*
No serf who pays gentle homage and receives his
*   supper in return.*
I have always dreamed of love bordering on
*   madness,*
*   Not settled instead in decency and logic.*
A curse on decency that strives to control what it
*   cannot love,*
*   And only loves what it cannot control.*
Mothers still insisting that their little boys comb their
*   hair*
*   And put the peanut butter jar back into the*
*   cupboard,*
Like altar boys still keeping all the rules, or boy scouts
*   Masquerading as men.*
Lust asking permission, rage taking out a permit,
Fear afraid to reveal itself,
*   Lest it lose what it never had.*

How Many Times

How many times have I looked at you
And wondered where you strayed,
Wondered to what memories you wandered
Or what secret hopes filled your heart,
Wondered in doubtful times if you wanted to leave
To find another life where only gentle chimes
echoed across the morning light,
And church bells rang triumphantly at midnight.
I know I bring a fractured love,
A heart pieced together at great cost,
Eyes scarred from too much seeing
And ears dimmed with a plethora of sounds.
I bring you a face marked by time's relentless
sculpting,
A memory circumscribed by joy and
disappointments,
A mind cluttered with unfinished plans
And half-completed hopes.
But most of all I only bring myself,
With all the love and courage and tenderness I
possess.
And I only fear when I look at you—withdrawn and
distant—
And wonder where you strayed.

I'm Gonna Sit Here

I'm gonna sit here
  Till passion returns
  And tells me where to go.
I don't care if it's heaven
  Or hell or home,
I don't care if it's work
  Or play or sex,
I don't care if it's rich
  Or poor or madness
I don't even care
  If it's riding a white horse naked on a
      freeway
  Or lining up like we did as kids
      For a pissing contest in the old
      schoolyard.
I'm not going anywhere
  —even to death—
Until I can go passionately.

To Begin Again

There are days when I want to begin again,
To be that smiling, secretly lonely boy who
  struggled to please an entire world.
I still see him in school, hand raised, shaking
  fiercely like some new flag begging to be
  recognized.
I see him walking shyly from school on a crisp
  winter afternoon,
Longing to be attractive and noticed, hungering
  to be held and touched,
But content instead to smile and make the
  basketball team.
Most of all I remember carmel breasts pressed
  against a white silk blouse, drooping eyelids and
  a perfect face,
The soft brown hair and woman's musical voice,
  a head taller than I was, rich and poised and
  sophisticated beyond all my abilities.
She was the real source of all my beginning
  fears, the vortex of my self-doubts.
Had I the courage to tell her that I loved her,
  that the very color and texture of her skin
  excited me, that her body was designed to
  dissolve with mine, that every word from her lips
  or slow smile
Touched me at some strange merging place of
  body and spirit,
Perhaps I would never have had to prove myself
  worthy of a hundred loves I really didn't want.
Even now, though a lifetime has passed, I remember
  every facet of her face, every crevice of her body,
  every movement of her arms and legs,

And now I can see that she loved me as much as I
loved her, wanted me as instinctively as I
wanted her—probably still does in the fibers of
consciousness that come and go like silent ghosts
of another life.
Only a few times have I seen her since childhood, but
curiously nothing has changed,
And I can only wonder if facing that first and most
threatening fear
Would not have made empty shadows of all the rest.

Some Darkness Descends

Some darkness descends tonight that I have never
known before,
A darkness unquenchable by sun or stars, a
prison with narrow walls and barred doors that
forbid me to see the light of the tiniest candle on
a child's birthday cake.
I who roamed forests till the trees sang melodies
unwritten by any master,
Who crossed rivers on mossy rocks and fell
sprawling into silent pools hidden from all but
chosen friends,
Am now forbidden the sky, fearful to ask a
stranger directions, afraid to find my way across
a familiar street grown unfamiliar.
My strength is gone, my eyes grow dim, no music
can restore peace to my soul.
I who wanted everything tonight have nothing.
I who sought to cross the world and sing to it my
joyful and melancholy songs have become as
nothing.
I am a poet without an audience, a desperate
man who cannot find the key to his desolation.
Is there an answer for such as me, a way out, a
home for a man who has abandoned every home
he ever owned?
My beauty fades, my soul withers, and the marks of
time tell me that soon there will be nothing left of
me but an assemblage of dust.
Only love is left, and without it,
Some darkness descends tonight that I have never
known before.

In My Town

In my town
Dogs have far more rights
than most people.
Few of us can yell at night
without reproach
And keep swearing poets
on the verge of murdering dogs.
Every time I see a policeman
Stop a kid with a backpack
and put him through a search
and seize
for dope or stolen
silverware, I
presume,
I wonder when the marauding policeman
Arrested his last dog.
No backpacked kid ever kept me awake all
night.

It's All Wrong Somehow

It's all wrong somehow
Cars trudging along freeways,
Joggers running nowhere
All in the name of health and progress.
So much sameness and dullness and
mediocrity
So much sadness and silence and
hypocrisy.
Even Joe's Cafe has surrendered to McDonald's
and Burger King
Where we can safely assume that the food
is never bad—
Or really good,
Food without surprises as tasteless and
dull as too many lives.
Maybe the Pied Piper will appear to lure the
joggers away
To a world that does not stagger minds
and waste bodies,
And tell those choking along the crowded
freeways
That a sailing ship leaves tomorrow for
Singapore.
Finally to rip away the sameness of TV and
condos
And millions of lives that have sacrificed
Freedom for affluence
Surprises for safety and sameness,
Even as a personalized computer promises
us more progress
And less privacy and significance.

No wonder the young skate along sidewalks lost
*   in their earphones,*
No wonder the old are lost in their TVs,
*   dreaming of guesting on a gameshow.*
It's all wrong somehow
*   Cars trudging along freeways*
*   Joggers running nowhere*
All in the name of health and progress!

The Book Burners

Well, the book burners are out in force these days,
Not worried so much about Darwin and Freud—who
    must be chagrined to be old hat so soon,
But worrying instead about Steinbeck, The Merchant
    of Venice, and wily old Huckleberry Finn,
Attacking indecent language and racial slurs,
Unmindful that most healthy people speak indecent
    language on important occasions like love and
    hate and varying shades of exuberance or
    surprise,
Unaware that racial and sexual slurs are still a
    significant part of every culture and aren't
    eradicated by banning the books that reflect the
    way things are.
But I suppose Dante must go with his biased
    assignments to heaven and hell
Only to be certainly followed by Mencken, Shaw,
    Nietzsche, Voltaire, and, of course, a
    revilification of Ulysses and Henry Miller.
Assuredly the bible must not be overlooked with
    Josue's sadism and David's adultery, not to
    mention Paul's attitude towards Jews,
    Corinthians, homosexuals, and women.
And Christ's own blatant anarchy and attacks on the
    moral majority.
I presume Little Women is safe, though it does portray
    feminine stereotypes, while even Tom Sawyer
    supports laziness and lies and noxious attitudes
    towards Indians.
The Little Engine That Could is a direct attack on
    railroads,

And Dickens' Christmas Carol *makes the rich seem
heartless and greedy.*
Mother Goose *is probably pornographic,* Br'er Rabbit
*is racist, and Aesop is unquestionably a
Communist.*
*I presume Dr. Seuss is not yet seen as subversive and
Chaucer will survive because the censors can't
understand him.*
*Nixon's memoirs are safe and the Harlequin
Romances sell like cereal.*
But meanwhile I'm rewriting Little Black Sambo *so
that a white kid discovers a psychotic tiger, takes
him to the zoo, and shares his pancakes made
from all natural ingredients, thus rendering him
a harmless pussycat.*
*So far the censors have not attacked me—nor the
nutritionists—nor even the animal lovers—not
to mention the book burners.*
*The problem is: I just can't get the damn boring thing
published!*

Well, the Real Estate Market Broke Down

Well, the real estate market broke down
And a lot of egos with it.
Paper castles came tumbling down, seaweed security
That made us laugh at our fathers' struggles to
survive.
All blew away in some sudden wind from far across
the globe.
Suddenly it was enough to have a house and a
family, a tree,
And a warm place by the fire.
Suddenly love meant more than all the trophies
And accumulated equities.
So much energy spent in vacuums, so much strength
locked in file cabinets.
So little time spent in forests
And in the quietude of our souls!

I Wonder about Derek

I wonder about Derek
  With all of his bachelor talk about prime sex and
    multiple orgasms,
  Assorted beds and new stimulants,
    and freedom despite herpes,
  Of liberating love so available
    in chance meetings and vagrant arms.

I wonder about the loneliness in his eyes
  The emptiness of leave-taking
    in the morning
  As he heads out for new, exciting conquests and
    fresh appetizers,
  Setting himself up for more excitement
    with the ensuing letdowns.

I wonder if sex is as good and satisfying as he says
  Or if he's just another kind of junkie
    with his fix
  That doesn't fix anything very long,
    but yearns for more,
  And each startling novelty of strange flesh
    only makes love more impossible.

I wonder if sex has not become a hype
  To replace warmth and caring,
  A commercial to keep us confused
    about what life offers,
  An obsessive diversion for those
    impoverished ones who never rest in
    the arms of a sunset

Or make quiet love, hand-in-hand,
watching a bold moon disappear
behind clouds.

Most of all I wonder about Derek
His lonely eyes
His restless energy
His sadness in repose
And all his bachelor talk about "prime sex."

Moose

Moose has an obnoxious way
  Of standing too close when he talks
  And grabbing my lapel so I don't drift
    away
    Like everyone always does,
  Or he takes a breath in the middle of a
    sentence
  And leaves no room at the end
  To terminate his monologue.
Lately, for whatever reason,
  I have taken some new initiative.
  When Moose stands too close,
    I stand closer.
  When he grabs my lapel,
    I grab his.
It's really hard to be boring
  At that distance,
  With interlocking arms grabbing lapels.

Teddy

There's every reason for Teddy
To lie down and die.
 His business folded
 His wife left him
 His home will be owned by the bank in a
  month
 He badly needs dental work he can't afford
 Young women don't notice him anymore
 His confident gait has been reduced to a
  slow shuffle
 His friends don't call
 The newspaper promises it will get worse
 Only his dog seems loyal
  And even he struggles to get up with
  bad arthritis.
Of course, there's every reason to lie down and die,
 But what would his grandson think?
 And where would he go if he left the earth
  And discovered that things were as bad
  somewhere else?
Meanwhile, he just hangs on,
 Enjoying a smoke
 Coffee in the morning
 The sun filtering through his one-room
  apartment,
 Grateful for a dog and a grandson
Who care about nothing that he has or doesn't have,
 Nothing that he's done or hasn't done,
But only that he's still Teddy.

Winfield Scott Ph.D.

Winfield Scott Ph.D. told me quite confidentially
    Over stoneground corn chips and margaritas
That enough M&Ms and electric shocks,
    Through operant conditioning
    And negative reinforcement
Could transform a hardened criminal
    Into a God-fearing man.
Mrs. Scott assured me that candy kisses
    Would work just as well.
I wondered how we turned God-fearing men
    Into human beings.
Winfield smiled vacantly and took the last corn chip.
    There were no M&Ms.

I Will Trust a Civilization

I will trust a civilization
  When old men
      Have a wise and confident look
  And old women
      Look gentle and cared for.
  When the eyes of the young
      Are diffident
          And filled with hope.
I will always be saddened
  By defeated old men and broken women
      And the arrogant eyes
  Of the young.

I Really Like Those Letters

I really like those letters that come with
　　"Dear Sir: How would you like to be enrolled
　　In a Group Policy by Allstate
　　　　For accidental death and
　　　　　　dismemberment—
　　Either you or your entire family?"
My God! How the hell would he or she,
　　Or even Mrs. Allstate like to be enrolled?
I get this funny picture of being clothes-lined by a
　　semi,
　　With my arms and legs rolling down the freeway,
　　And what's left of me is screaming joyously:
　　　　"Thank God for my dismemberment policy!"
Or I see this funny man at his desk,
　　With a Dustin Hoffman smile on a Steve Martin
　　　　face,
　　Cutting up paper figurines into assorted
　　　　dismemberments,
　　As he licks the stamps to solicit other members
　　To be dismembered. Shouting all the while:
"Ah, there goes an ear and three teeth!"
"Oh boy! A hand in the garbage disposal, a foot in a
　　bear trap,
　　Or an eye in a wide-open frisbee contest!"
But the part I like best is the computerized:
　　"Respond by August 15 to guarantee early
　　　　processing of enrollment!"
Sounds like college, or dance school, or a free trip to
　　Singapore.
　　"Not a moment's least delay! You can be
　　　　dismembered today!"
　　Valium anyone?

I Have Always Loved You

I have always loved you
With oblique and hidden glances,
Not so much the times you were on parade,
But twilight on the beach
When you did not know I was
gazing at you.
And late at night
When you dozed from TV,
cradled against my shoulder.
It was then I thanked a complicated, confusing
world
That you were mine and I yours,
Walking together through forests
And along the silver edge of
dark rivers,
Drifting wordlessly along
beaches
And skiing leisurely down
blinding bowls of snow,
Watching late movies and
cuddling against the cold,
Dancing in little cafés and
laughing at midnight,
Then turning suddenly silent
without permission.
Always holding you close at night like an
innocent child,
Forever peeking at you when you
didn't notice,
And loving you immeasurably with oblique and
hidden glances.

Without You

Without you, I make no sense of clouds circling the
    sky like protective angels,
Guarding the world and its inhabitants from all
    harm.
Without you, I do not wonder at the relentless waves
    following one another like eternal sighs
Heaving heavenward and echoing mightily across the
    earth.
Without you, there is no morning, no sunset, no
    laughing trees and breathless winds,
No friendly shadows dancing on moonlit nights.
Without you there are no whining gulls begging for
    food, no pelicans, sedate and wise,
Surveying the silent waters and guarding their
    prehistoric secrets.
Without you, there are no brooding mountains
    crowned with snow like wrinkled old men,
And gazing patiently at the troubled valleys.
Without you, there are no soundless stars grazing like
    silver sheep in an endless meadow,
No sun to transform the dying leaves from grey to
    gold.
Without you, the squirrels do not chatter in oak trees,
    the doves do not mourn from rooftops,
The plump quail do not scream and scamper across
    the fields.
Without you, I am an orphaned child, trembling on a
    darkened street in an unfamiliar city,
And calling your name to all the locked and silent
    houses.
Without you, I am Cain and cursed to wander, I am
    finally homeless and joyless and all alone,
Without you.

Nothing Has Changed from Childhood

Nothing has changed from childhood,
*   The same longing for peace,*
*   The same hope for final fulfillment.*
Life could have been easier had there been teachers
*   and wise men instead of drones imitating*
*   drones and parrots mimicking parrots.*
If I were to begin again, I would challenge authority
*   from the crib,*
*   Trust only smiles and laughter that echo across*
*   all darkness.*
For years I puzzled over monks who left the world to
*   hide in cloisters and ancient regulations.*
At last I know that freedom is a curse save for the very
*   brave,*
*   And I am only brave enough to wonder at the*
*   heavens.*
Too many friends have died, too many stars are
*   fallen,*
Too many questions go unanswered.
Philosophers waste their time, even Augustine was
*   grave too soon.*
I would have loved him before his conversion.

There is too much pain in the world,
*   Too much suffering without significance,*
*   Till finally I know that love alone is worth the*
*   price,*
*   Yet no one told me about love.*

I was taught that conquests would fill the emptiness
beneath the surface of my heart.
Now I am content to be Aesop, selling my fables for
lunch money,
Satisfied to avoid black holes and galaxies,
Staying close to frogs and flowers and the smell
of baking bread.
I wander the slums of Beijing and Brazil, and know
that staying alive is joy enough when the struggle
is too fierce.
I woke this morning, wondering what was left to do,
asking questions which only I can answer,
Finally grateful to love with a wounded heart.
So, for today, I will survive, and for tomorrow,
Because nothing has changed from childhood,
Except I no longer permit anyone beyond myself
To tell me what to do.

Computer Living

In the morning, after reading the paper left
    mysteriously outside my hotel room, wrapped in
    "Have a good day!"
I put my green card in the money machine and was
    welcomed graciously to the Valley Bank, saw my
    name in print, and received $100 in twenties
    without a word to anyone.
Later I opened my mail only to be congratulated by a
    computerized letter with eight personal
    references and nine reasons why I should
    consider solar power in a house I was
    remodeling.
I paid a few bills on the phone to a computerized
    voice with the patience of a nut waiting for a
    bolt, and was thanked with the gentle inflection
    of software.
I called a wrong number and a codified larynx set
    me straight, not once, but four times without
    rancor.
I selected my food in a computerized automat with no
    tipping,
Played six games of Pac Man with music and no one
    cheating,
Returned to my hotel room where I ordered the next
    day's breakfast by the numbers,
Dialed four digits for a movie which was to be
    codified into my final bill which I paid without
    waiting in line or talking to anyone.
Only then did I realize that I had spent twenty-four
    hours without human contact, save for a maid
    who offered more towels.

Somewhat distraught, I wandered down the street
and imagined a world where everyone could go
for days without talking, touching, or seeing
another human being.
I was two-thirds of the way through the development
of a complex system of computerized sex and
massage parlors,
When a well-dressed beggar told me he was down on
his luck and needed a bus ride to Pittsburgh to
visit his dying mother.
As I fumbled in my wallet for the fare, he informed
me politely that he also took Visa and Master
Charge.

To My Lonely Friend

Lonely man, finally all alone
With the fragments of your life
Scattered like an angry, frightened puzzle.
Only a few friends left, the chosen ones,
Who can look beyond your despair
And remember a gentle laugh.
Who can look beyond a thousand fears
And remember a quiet courage,
Who look beyond success and achievements
To a face, eyes, a generous heart.
Tonight, when you cannot walk another step
Or hang on to anything within you,
I will hang on to you one more day,
Hoping against all hope
That this pain and confusion and fear will end,
Hoping that total darkness
Will be relieved by the flicker of any light.
It will get clearer soon.
Life is all there is to hang on to,
And life seems to have deserted you finally.
Yet, you have endured another day,
And do not forget two or three fleeting moments
of joy.
Hold on to life, my friend, to life, to life!
It is the gift!
Hold on to life, even feebly for one more day,
If not for yourself,
For those of us who love you!

When the Pain Is More Acute Than You Can Bear

When the pain is more acute than you can bear,
And you are convinced that no one in the world
  suffers as much,
When the morning is as opaque as night and the
  dawn but a discordant alarm, announcing yet
  another bitter struggle to survive,
When a bird's song to the day or the serene
  murmuring of a dove
  Cannot draw your mind from feeding on itself,
Clinging like some wretched scavenger to drain out
  joy and wonder,
When the soft light of daybreak cannot distract or the
  gentle shimmering of the locust leaves cannot
  inspire,
When even the shrill cries of summer children are but
  screams that echo in some mad corridor of
  consciousness,
Know that you are not dying, but preparing to enter
  another level of life,
A level beyond avarice and fleeting fame, beyond
  servile dependence on opinions or words of
  praise,
Beyond power and mastery and control, beyond
  jealousy and competition,
Beyond lust and greed and insatiable ambition, a
  level where joy flows from simplicity and love,
From some rhythm shared with trees and flowers and
  circling planets.

Then all the pain is as nothing, rather a choice and
heavenly messenger sent like some ancient angel
of the East
To announce a more profound and solid way to self-
esteem and serenity.
Thus pain is not an enemy, but a friend who promises
to take you where peace abides,
Who leads you beyond bitterness to abandon specious
and empty pursuits, hollow and ill-founded
hopes, destructive and untimely dreams,
Until you walk in the world freer and more joyful
than ever before,
Less anxious and less frightened of death, one with
life,
In an harmonious accord,
Bred of suffering, of annihilation,
Bred of emptiness and frustration,
And leading directly and inexorably to a true and
genuine,
An eternal and purified self.

Priest

Tall and straight
With a giant head in the heavens
And feet planted solidly on earth.
A man who cares about the whole world,
Rages with rebels in El Salvador
And jousts with popes in Poland,
To whom Lebanon is as close as Los Angeles,
And Nicaragua as familiar as San Francisco.
A man mad enough to reach out,
To see beyond symbols and love beyond words,
To walk in narrow places, still in touch with the
sun.
A priest, whose altar is the universe,
Whose liturgy extends from vagrants to the stars,
Whose theology begins with God and ends with
human hearts,
Whose sacraments are wisdom and laughter and
unending exploration.
A man brave enough to be afraid,
Real enough to know pain,
And to know as well it is not forever.
A friend, who's there when lonely days and
nights descend,
Whose home is as open as his heart,
A priest, a man, an artist, and a chosen friend,
Whose very being is his greatest work of
art.

Finding the Courage

Finding the courage to face some buried anxiety
   As real as snakes and grizzly bears in an
      uncharted wilderness,
Struggling in vain to recall a child's overpowering
   fear
   Still rooted deeply in my flesh
   And seemingly as impermeable as granite rocks.
When was that terrifying moment that has
   Left its shadows till now?
What was the dagger that carved a scar never to be
   erased?
   Was I seven or seventeen, infant or fragile
      adolescent?
Vainly I recall every angry, hurtful voice of childhood,
   Every silent attack of parent or peer, teacher or
      coach.
Who wounded me when my bones were too brittle to
   bear the weight?
   When my mind was too timid and unformed to
      fight back?
How can I battle this elusive Hydra
   With its hybrid and devouring teeth?
Will I carry the last of this struggle to my grave?
   Will it reappear to torture me at the very end?
Or will the sun finally rise some glorious morning
   And the roots of an ancient fear dissolve like the
      disappearing night?

Peace

In a complex and oft confusing world,
When life's details
        Get in the way of living,
And mounting worries
Crowd out simple beauty
        Of snow and silence,
        Fresh water and flowers,
When tragedy strikes without warning
And suffering arrives unannounced,
Then most of all
        We must cling to what is truly beautiful:
        Children, love, laughter, dreams,
        Wisdom, wonder, all that friendship means,
Rearranging priorities, and taking time
        To discover what is alien,
        What is really mine.
'Tis then confusion softens, storms cease,
'Tis then descends the gift of private peace.
May such peace surround our lives
        And fill our space,
May peace transform our hearts
        And thus our race.

Laughing at Mary

For years the whole neighborhood
    laughed at Mary
        With her dyed red hair and fifty extra
            pounds
        Her tight skirts and beads around her neck,
        Her rouge and clacking teeth and novenas
            all in place,
        Her rosaries and holy water and a dozen
            saints all promising to protect her.
Well a lot of time has gone by
    and Mary hasn't changed much.
But Sid next door died of cancer,
Bart in the stone house on the corner,
    lost a fortune in real estate,
Wally at the end of the block is finally
        alcoholic
And Dave across the street had a triple bypass.
Benny the bartender's wife left him
    with no one to listen to his jokes anymore.
Now only the very, very young and unaware laugh at
    Mary
        With her rouge and rosaries,
        Her dyed red hair and fifty extra pounds.

Yesterday I Questioned

Yesterday, I questioned the leisure born of
    affluence
    That allows me to wonder what life
        means.
And I cursed the education that rescued me
    From the simple faith of my forebears,
    And the comforting superstitions of an
        aging peasant.
There are times like today
    When it would be nice to know
        That three Hail Marys could heal me,
        A novena or nine Fridays could give
            me hope,
        Or even the innocent blood of a
            chicken, shed on an ancient
            Irish hillside long before Christ,
        Could free me from some bottomless
            guilt.
But no matter what I may feel of angels or
    devils,
    Or trembling hands clutching at wrinkled
        rosary beads,
They sure as hell beat unending self-analysis.

The Demons

The demons of morning came to tell me that my
    life was over,
    That fears buried in childhood would
        haunt me all my life.
I rose up early to fight with all my strength to love the
    flowers
    Because I knew that life was on my side,
        and if I could but cling to it long enough,
    I would survive.
I feared helpless poverty, that my talent had
    disappeared,
    That no one would ever love me.
I turned to God Whom I had forgotten,
    Even though thousands said He let each
        make his own way
    Amid the angry protons and neutrons
        ready to dissolve the earth.
I clung to the sun and the mountains, the distant
    love of a woman,
    The memory of a child and the mystery of
    a little boy's smile.
Still the demons, relentless in their assault, sought
    hungrily
    To overrun me,
But I knew somehow that if I did not look back or
    even forward,
    I could endure if only hour by hour, day
    by day.
There was no solace in the world, nor even in the
    suffering
    Of so many whose pain was far more
    critical than mine.

I knew instinctively that love and passion must fill my
*   heart,*
*   Truth must envelop my soul, and I must*
*   reach out to others who needed my help.*
And then if I were to be destroyed, it would be
*   destiny's decree,*
*   And not because fear and shadows had*
*   overcome the sun.*
How long can one fight without victory?
How long can elusive fears make a mockery of all
*   I have become?*
I knew there must be a place on earth for me
*   If only to make another happy*
*   And to interpret my world as best I could.*
Once I rose up early and rejoiced in simple beauty.
*   I had to believe that I would do it again.*
If he chose ignorant fishermen to do his work,
*   there must*
*   Be a place for me, cast from the garden,*
*   cut off from the simple formula of*
*   most men's lives.*
I am only afraid, terribly afraid, not dying,
*   and I will not*
*   Live on pills and empty promises,*
But on the painful reality that what is, is.

The Monks Pray

The monks pray while the city sleeps,
The city wakes while the monks still pray.
The monks still sing their ancient, magic words,
While I must ponder what there is to say
To an unknown God Who guards the nameless birds
And knows the things I need before I pray.
Perhaps it is enough to let my silence speak,
To leave the monks their psalms and chiseled words,
For I am but the least among the weak,
Another frightened, lonely, nameless bird.

More Complicated

I know the trembling economy has to be more
  complicated than a mediocre carpenter charging
  $20 an hour
And a mechanic diagnosing my sick car for $73, a
  special rate,
"Which coulda been $120" if he had really charged
  for his time.
Certainly the economy is more complicated than
  waiting for an assistant painter for an hour to
  return from his break—and a roofer working
  half a day when I'm not watching.
And certainly as a born democrat raised poor
  I know that the unions rescued man from slavery
    so that he could gain enough equality
    finally to make a fool of management and
    me, and latterly himself.
So, of course the troubled economy has got to be
  Russians and Arabs or immigrants, developers or
  brokers, or Taiwan and Japan,
And assuredly not everyone in the country wanting
  everything
  Without working hard for it,
  Or being proud of it,
  Or giving a damn about anything except how
    much they get,
Which will soon enough mean nothing, because it is
  nothing,
  And so's everything else that doesn't make you
    feel you earned it—honestly, by your own
    effort.
But, of course, it's got to be far more complicated
  than that.

Scott

Scott's one of those kids
  Everyone laughs at and parents worry about
  Eleven going on five,
  With gentleness and tenderness nobody grades at
    school.
He's still playing with toys in the bathtub,
  Still drifting through a magic world
    Where clouds are fuzzy messengers
    And stars are blinking code-lights
    from another world.
He is not harsh enough to live,
  Too gracious ever to be rude,
  Too innocent ever to succeed,
  Too beautiful to be understood,
  Too fragile and loving to compete with anyone.
His eyes are dreamy enough to see the heart of trees
  And the soft core of rocks,
Ears sensitive enough to hear the music of rainbows
  And the delicate rhythm of the wind.
Friend of caterpillars and ants, bees and chickadees,
  Ladybugs, sea shells, and squeaking field mice.
He hears too many sounds to concentrate on one,
  Too many voices to pay attention,
Sees too many visions to focus on a blackboard.
He is the unrewarded symbol of life beyond the skies,
The chosen messenger of wonder and surprise.
Doomed to fail beyond all obvious measure of success,
Destined to succeed where the prize is happiness.

Recently

Recently I attended a seminar where liberated
    women taught unresisting men how to be proper
    mates,
And sequestered couples wrote wordy notes to make
    certain they'd been heard.
Nobody swore, shouted, drank too much, or
    fantasized sex that began in formal dress and
    ended with laughing and loving and nude
    wrestling in an old mill pond.
    Which is what I really wanted to slip into my
        brief, sequestered note.
Later, we were catechized in the rights of boys to play
    with dolls,
    And of grown men to cry at least twice a week.
    (Even though no boy of mine would dress a doll
    And males weeping twice a year would send
        most women looking for a mate who could
        hold it together.)
Little was said to help women understand that a man
    is more than a hairy, laconic, flat-chested
    woman.
And now that pubs, clubs, and massage parlors are
    communal, I am looking for a seminar that
    accepts men without squeezing their feelings into
    cardiac arrest.
Wondering all the while what it would be like for a
    boy to grow up
    Without a role model who is often gruff, raucous,
        bigoted, unshowered and unshaven,
    And as tender as any woman in the world.
I finally concluded that with the massive pressure to
    redefine sex,

The skinny kid with sand in his eyes walks off
with the bikini,
Leaving the muscleman to his dolls.
The skinny kid, of course, won't unsnap the
lady's bra without permission,
So she does it herself, removes his shorts, and
directs him
How and when she wants to be loved.
And if all else fails, there's that seminar where
liberated women
Teach unresisting men how to be proper mates.

All My Life

All my life
I thought love was earned
By how I looked
Or what I accomplished
How cleverly I spoke
Or how I could make people laugh.
So all my life
I worried about my appearance
Or some new conquest
The force of my words
Or the jokes I could tell.
Somehow I've discovered
In these latter days
That love is a gift
Given lavishly without recompense
Freely beyond bargaining or good sense
Totally without concern for expense.
Only earning it is impossible.

How I Long for You

How I long for you
When my whole being turns upside down,
When all the fears of a lifetime gather
    in a single, uninvited attack
And paralyze my most intense will,
When a single, unexpected touch from you, an
    unsolicited kiss, a smile, a spontaneous word of
    love
Would make me know for a time that all the pain is
    somehow worthwhile.
Only love seems to make it all bearable
    As I struggle to hang on to a passing cloud.
Only love can create final healing as I whisper my
    terror to the wind.
Only love can undo what wounds and violence and
    time have done.
Only love can transform this abiding fear into
    sustaining life and wholeness.
And thus, like a child lost in the dark allies of a
    massive city too confusing and frightening,
I long for you, not to save me,
But only to love me as no one ever has.

Couples Gathered

Couples gathered in social settings
Bored with the monotony of their own routines,
*   Sniffing new aromas*
*   Fondling new fantasies*
*   And hiding the hurt especially from each other.*
Too timid to make a move
*   Beyond handsies and footsies*
*   And ring-a-round the eyesies.*
Obliged to live out their lives
*   Conforming to worn-out dreams*
*   In fear of revealing what each already knows.*
Finally unaware that this is the only life
*   They'll ever have.*

Love-Making Time Again

Love-making time again
With all the rote signs of erotic boredom,
Hands probing dotted lines in darkness,
An infant's hands begging a parent to
drive dragons away.
She awaits listlessly his timid assault grown
drab as her response,
Feigns beginning sleep, waits as if she
hasn't heard his silent whine.
Nervously he touches her, then feebly again.
She touches back
Like a cow that must reluctantly be
milked,
Resigned before a neighbor's
baby that must be changed.
He shifts his body
Whining like a stray cat that
must be stroked and fed,
Then groans his spasm of thanks like
the dull echo
Of a blank cartridge in a
shooting gallery,
Then rolls over like a well-fed hound dog.
Now she is more fully awake,
Stroking her fantasy lamp for a lean and
confident lover,
Who will not grovel for the dullest
kneading
Or acknowledge sullenness with a
child's pleading.

"I will leave him soon," she sighs.
 (The thrill is gone after a dozen years.)
"I will leave her soon," he lies.
 (The dulled victim of a thousand fears.)

Love-making time again
 With familiar signals of erotic boredom
 Clinging to what's at hand for fear of
  losing everything,
  Knowing instinctively that
The streets are too dark and dangerous for
  broken lives,
That lean and confident lovers
 Scurry from scarred husbands and angry,
  wounded wives.

Those Truths

Those truths you seem so sure of,
  Somehow don't seem like yours.
And the words you spout so easily
  Remind me of how things were
When prophets told me what to feel
  And experts what to say,
When high priests decided what was real,
  And gurus knew the way.
Latterly I've learned to wonder
  To withhold my final belief.
Secretly I pity Judas,
  And admire the unrepentant thief.

I Saw You

I saw you as a beloved, phantom child
Beyond all years or time's reckoning,
And would have given all that I am
To possess your eyes.
Damn time's insolence
To enumerate all the years I never
noticed.
Now I must wonder
About the passing of years
And the counting of hours,
Wonder
If a gnarled tree
Can love spring's flowers.

Life Stretches Ahead

Life stretches ahead
Like some uncharted, winding gravel road
    Passing through hills and valleys
With unfamiliar scenery and disappearing
    landmarks.
Even loyal friends who have seen me through
    madness and mounting fears
    Cannot tell me which way to turn
    Or when to turn back at the threat of
    sudden storms.
Even my lover struggles to survive and cannot
    whisper comforting directions
    When dawn bursts on my consciousness,
    confusing me with its exaggerated
    splendor,
    Or darkness calms my torrent of fright,
    permitting me a momentary peace.
So I walk, step by step,
    Guided by sometimes friendly stars
    Washed by the wind and rain
    Chilled by the snow of mountain peaks
    Warmed by the desert's monotonous heat,
Trusting blindly that the gravel road will take
    me where I must go,
Hoping quietly that the unfamiliar scenery is
    only a friend dressed differently,
Loving gently all I meet along the way
    Where none who walks alone is ever a
    stranger,
As life stretches ahead.

My God!

My God! I am weary of being a fragile, dried
  tree,
That flames so easily from a casual spark
  Thrown unwittingly from a careless
   camper or passing car.
Where are the rains I stored amid years of
  unrecorded pain
  And silent tears,
  Rains enough to cool any fire in the
   world,
  Rains certainly enough to smother
   smoldering words?
Why did you ever love me,
  Tease me with your dulcet flattering?
Why did I ever make public my secret thoughts
  To endure your fiery tongue that
   devoured my leaves
   And licked my branches clean?
Professional critics are but complacent
  vultures
  Who claw but do not char my bark.
You burn and blister because I thought you
  loved me,
  Knew me, touched my very soul.
Thus your words became the most cruel and
  ravaging of all,
  Burning like a sudden forest fire beyond
   control,

Scorching my heart and soul,
Leaving me charred and desolate as if
spring would never come,
And only a savage winter could
mercifully hide the scars.
Strange, I thought you but one spark amid the
thousands,
A harmless firefly I could gather in a
bottle like a child.
But I let you love me and tell me so with
glowing words,
And like a fool gave you the power to
crush me.

The Time Came

The time came when all that is merely human failed,
And the best efforts of medics and wise men with
all the tools of two thousand years of trying
Came to nought. I was cut adrift from myself, destined
to wither
If I could not salvage a suitable reason to live,
Finally cut off from the omnipotence of parental help,
Finally segregated from the abundant generosity of
friends,
Finally having exhausted the relief that the centuries
had garnered from the vials and occult theories
of civilization's finest minds.
There were no relieving drugs or miracles, no
soothing words enough or clever theorems.
Only the simple words I heard as a child of a God
Who cared
And could make a blind man see for no reason
save love.
So I sought Him in simplicity and fear, perhaps in
desperation,
More in doubt than faith, more in faltering
words than bold eloquence.
I offered Him my energies all the days of my life if He
would but attend my pleading, bring back the
joy of morning, the serenity of the trees, the
soothing resonance of sunset.

I asked not fame or power, security or success, only
the wholeness that every other recourse had
denied me.
Softly He spoke, not in Sinai's thunder or Noe's rain,
not in transcending light upon a mountain, nor
even in a whispered call along the shores of
Galilee.
He only spoke of patience and enough time, of
listening to the day and attending the night,
That wholeness would come when my heart was pure
again,
And my aspirations were those of a child grown to
manhood.

Everyone Listens

Everyone listens to your pain for awhile,
    Some out of curiosity
    Some relieved that you are not too strong
    Some for money, which seems to make it easier
        to listen.
But even friends grow weary of hearing the same old
    pain.
    So do the curious
    And the compassionate
    Even wives and well-paid doctors.
Finally we all end up talking silently to ourselves.
And maybe the healing takes place
    When even we are bored.

Don't You Know

Don't you know
    That lovers make the rains,
    Call forth the sun,
    Re-route hurricanes,
    And exorcise earthquakes for fun.

Don't you know
    That lovers dissipate tornadoes,
    Rearrange the clouds,
    Manufacture moonlight,
    In silence away from crowds.

Alas, my friend,
    You listen too well to hear,
    Unaware that only love can last forever.
    You've become a barometer of fear,
    Resigned reluctantly to accept the weather.

Nights Without You

Nights without you
  Are like streetlights
  On a deserted corner in childhood.
If only you were a room away
  Or I could hear you puttering in the kitchen
I would be as warm and comfortable
  As cradled in your arms.
Now I am afraid to tell you that I die without you
  Lest my urgency frighten you away like a shy
    child.
Once I could wander the world for months
  With only the ever-present thought of you.
Watch midnight barbering in eerie streets of Old
  Jerusalem
Or drink to bulging belly dancers in the slums of
  Beirut.
Tonight I am afraid to walk across the room
  Lest I die of some recent loneliness.
I will be strong again soon
  And free to toast a lonely drunk in Cairo at
    dawn.
But for now, this night without you
  Is a strange and fearful solitude
Garnered from the loneliest corner of my boyhood.

Bertha

Her eyes are never far from
tears or laughter,
Her arms ready to touch and hold
and promise peace.
Her voice like a soothing wind,
strong and soft and ancient.
She is overweight, without makeup,
Grey before her time and generous
beyond all counting.
Most of all her love, enduring and practical,
ready to feed the hungry
or comfort the battered
Without thought of time or energy
or financial security.
No weak pollyanna too effeminate
for judgment or wisdom,
But unafraid of pain or tragedy,
and not doing for others
what they must do for themselves.
Somehow a friend of anyone in need
And proof that a God still walks the earth
in the person of this noble woman
Whose eyes are never far from
tears or laughter.

Well, I Read

Well, I read about what all the successful men
    are doing—and some women,
Accomplishing at thirty what I could never do in a
    lifetime,
Holding the world at attention and filled with
    every confidence.
Meanwhile, I rise filled with fear that I've done
    nothing, will do nothing, can do nothing,
Struggling one more time to believe that simply
    to be is what it's all about, but afraid a private
    sunset can't compare with Betamax and a
    Mercedes.
I reach for God Who is forever elusive and has
    few opinions about computers and hot tubs—but
    I reach just the same.
I reach for my beloved, wishing she could bring it all
    together for me, like some omnipotent mother,
But knowing too well that she can only try to
    understand my fear and love me—love me now
    more than ever before.
There is so much love needed in a dry and
    frightened world,
So much love in my heart, longing to be given,
    though I scarcely know where to give it.
So I begin the day with fear, struggling to still the fury
    of anxiety and indecision in a world
    I understand a little less each day,

Struggling to believe that all will come in time if I do
not lose patience and heart and courage.
Lo! The sun has risen, the day has already begun!
Gather your thread again, even a few strands,
and start the work that when finally begun will
grow apace in competition with no one,
Knowing that fear—though everywhere—is only
painful, and not dangerous.
Knowing that God—though everywhere—is only
distant, and not uncaring
Knowing that I—though weak and frightened—am
important to someone.

It's Time to Start Again

It's time to start again,
     Forget mistakes I've made
     And wounds inflicted
          By those who vowed to love me.
It's scary looking back
     At all the missed opportunities,
     The wrong roads,
     Hesitations that should have been decisions,
     Impulses that should have been slept on—for
          months.
Somehow I was infallible,
     My own Vatican,
     Sure of everything,
     Afraid of nothing,
     Confident that all would be as it ever was,
     Content with my collected platitudes when I
          wasn't hearing.
So much arrogance, so much ignorance,
     So much ingratitude, so much fury,
     So much struggling to get somewhere
          That I could ignore those who loved me.
A man rushing in every direction,
     Certain that some frantic move would bare life's
          secret,
     Or canonize him forever.

Now it's time to start again—slowly, cautiously,
Like a child examining the world for the very
first time,
Tired of seeing life at 32,000 feet or even 32,
Tired of seeing human pain and simple joy as
mere color patterns on a mad journey
to nowhere.
It's time to start again,
Quietly, lovingly, gratefully,
With time left over I never knew I had,
Time to see and hear
To be grateful, and finally,
To love.

If I Am Not as Strong as I Was

If I am not as strong as I was,
  Will you still love me?
If I am not as bold and brave,
  As self-assured and confident,
  As certain of my opinions
  And convinced of my power,
If I am tortured by fears
  That the dawn will dissipate like moonbeams,
If I am trembling and disheartened,
  As unsure as once I was infallible,
  As timid as once I was reckless,
Will you touch my face gently
  And measure the scars on my soul?
Will you hear the silence of my heart
  And the tension of my breathing?
Will you beyond all else
  Still love me?

Dale

Dale doesn't say much anymore
Living in dreams he almost knows
  Will never come to pass.
    His voice the echo of an empty cave
    His eyes a dark, moonless night,
    His expression a mountain in winter,
    His lips as thin and sad as a desert's
      horizon.
At times he's almost brave enough to admit
  He should have loved or left years ago,
  Knowing this was the only way to be free,
    But afraid to be who he is,
  Lest it be too little and she walk away
    And take away all the years of mothering.
He is still unaware that she would follow
  Where a strong man leads no matter the primal
    resistance,
Or wait patiently to attend him on his return from
    whatever war.
Instead, he remains silent, living in the darkness of
    dying dreams,
  Well aware that they will probably never come to
    pass
After all these years.

Louise

Louise thinks
I shouldn't take life so seriously,
That people with fewer brains
are a lot luckier,
And that people who think as deeply
as Louise thinks I sometimes do
Create their own misery, waste a lot of time,
And would be far better off having more kids,
Or even playing cribbage.

Louise also thinks
Her husband left her
Because her mother and the dog got on his
nerves,
The kids wrecked his saw and scratched his
Harley,
And it snowed too much in Chicago.

Louise and I are not close.

I Know

I know I should not lean on you,
That I should gather my strength
From past exploits and future dreams
From some inner vision or countless
triumphs.
But what happens when none of this works?
When praise is empty and joy a stranger
When even food is tasteless and my eyes
are too glazed
To appreciate the dawn or mallards
playing in a pond,
When my whole vision slumps into
distortions and voices
Echo like a mediocre movie on TV,
When only your eyes can see me, only
your words can reach me,
Only your touch is separate from my
own,
When you alone are my only real hope
In a suddenly frightening world?

Albert

Albert's easy smile and bellowing laugh
Tell you little about his life:
　Children grown and distant
　A wife departed with a close friend
　A God beyond hymns and self-
　　righteous codes
　A job undramatic and
　　unappreciated.

Now he has given into love,
　Dispensing it gently and generously
　　wherever he goes,
　Almost content to live alone
　　With books and music, tennis and
　　　golf,
　　Rock hounding and gold panning, a
　　　few friends,
　　And silence—lots of silence.
No one calls him noble and couragous,
No service club or civic committee
　Will ever acknowledge him.
And no one knows he's bleeding and wounded,
Because Albert's easy smile and bellowing laugh
Tell you little about his life.

Kept Woman

Kept woman with no more worries about food or roof,
With time to fondle your own ego till you die,
Time to explore paths never open to you before,
Time to work or not work, cook or not cook,
    Love or not love as fantasy and impulse
    direct.

Kept woman, protected by vows and lawyers,
    Affectionate in any direction you please, willing
    to humiliate or tease,
Without the honesty to admit what's happening.
Seductive men are everywhere, ready to wrap
    who will be wrapped,
    Lusting where it may lead, uncommitted
    and easily appeased by any victory.
Better they rush their victims to bed to discover if
    the odors are right.

Kept woman, are you not weary of distrust, weary of
    a love
    That is forever on stage, then goes its separate
    way in silence when the shades are drawn?
Are you not weary of seducers who succeed if
    only in their own minds?
And are you not weariest of all of denying what
    is really taking place?

Kept woman, love is not a local Gallup Poll,
    Nor is eternal adolescence
Worth the price of your very soul.

Great Guru

I think
I've finally lived long enough
To know
That the Great Guru in the sky
Ain't talking!

To Let Go

I long to let go, to release all the illusions
That separate me from what is,
To feel my body pulse and soar, lifting my mind from
its timidity and repairing all the ancient scars of
my soul,
To float through the day and dance into the night,
Following the directions of winds and clouds and
ever in touch with the earth.
To feel my roots descend into the deep waters of the
earth's core like a palm tree in the desert, strong
because it bends,
Unafraid because it flows with water and life.
I am not the solid, unshaken oak, I am leaves flying
from branches,
Scattered and helpless on the ground.
I am an evergreen, not high on a mountain, but
nestled in a valley by a stream, playing with
children,
Flying kites from my branches, loving the birds
that rest there,
Laughing in the sunshine and weeping softly in
the rain,
Letting go of all I ever aspired to be,
For I am already loved, and that alone is beyond
all illusion.

I Sometimes Remember

I sometimes remember amid the paper and the
    evening news
    That it was those powerful executives and
        politicians,
        Charming and insensitive,
        Logical and persevering,
        Confident and ruthless
Who built the cars we drive
    The planes and computers,
    Skyscrapers and hospitals,
    Space capsules and TVs
    Railroads and iron lungs and artificial hearts.
And I try to remember that they were probably not
    unlike
    The discoverers of new continents
    And the explorers of uncharted lands and
        unknown seas.
But I also remember that it was the same kind of men
    Stress-filled and calculating
    Unscrupulous and conniving
        Who started the pointless wars we fought
        The depressions and revolutions,
        The famines and slavery,
        The atrocities and plagues
        The poverty and starvation and private
            despair
            Of the fragile and
            disenfranchised.

Then I remember that it was the same kind of men
    —for whatever reason—
    Who ended the wars they began
    And solved the problems they created
    Even as they plotted to create even more.
All of which makes me wonder if we weren't better off
    Working by hand
    Traveling by foot
And listening to the music of the wind.

Woman-Child, Lost in Dreams

Woman-child, lost in dreams,
Wondering if they'll ever be fulfilled,
Scarred by time, wounded by love and
promises,
Afraid to try again.
Too gentle to build a wall around your heart,
Too warm to live a life apart,
Too loving not to pause—then start
again.
Have I told you that you walk above the earth?
That stars envy you and flowers blush
in your presence?
That all the wounds and pain will
cease
And you will be free and whole again?
Woman-child, lost in dreams
And wondering if they'll ever be
fulfilled,
Walk with me beyond the rivers and
the forests
And stand in naked loveliness on the
highest hill!
Woman-child!

In Memoriam: Three Years

My life will never be the same without you.
I smile, but not as broadly
I dream, but not as madly
I love, but not as deeply.
For I now know
That the river is not all it promised
And flowers are not everything they seem.
I will never see a flower again without
thinking of you.
Nor will I see the face of a man
As warm and sensitive as yours
Without inwardly dissolving in private
grief.
I do not weep anymore,
I have shed enough tears to water your flowers
forever.
But my life will never be the same without you.
Time is no healer, only a gentle friend who dulls
the surface pain and bids life go on.
This is my only obsequy, even for a man of your
nobility,
Who despite beloved flaws or unanswered
dreams
Has a friend, a brother
Who cannot accept the mercy of time's toll
To assuage what was forever a cruel and
untimely death
And who will never be the same without you.

So Much Pain

So much pain in human hearts,
So much hurt in human lives,
    Who gave me eyes to see so clearly?
    Who gave me ears to hear each inflection of
        terror?
    Who made me understand and feel the wounds
        of millions?
My God, Let me walk superficially through the world,
    Content to laugh with children
    Content to rejoice in the clouds
    Content to see the sun again and again and
        again.
I cannot endure nor understand the misery inflicted
    on mankind,
I cannot tolerate the bruises of so many.
My body aches tonight with a world's pain.
    I do not want to see one more tear,
    To hear one more tragedy,
    To know of another life dragged through misery
        beyond comprehension.
I only write
    To avoid the pain
    To escape finally the hurt
    To linger with the beauty that is everywhere in
        the world.
There are moments I want to explode,
    To be blasted to bits across the margents of the
        universe,
    To feel anything but my world's misery.
For now I will look to the moon
    Beyond my mountains
    Beyond my hurt
To heal the ache that will not leave me
    As long as I must listen to a screaming world.

Know This, My Friend

Know this, my friend,
I will never desert you.
I will be there when all have gone away,
When finally you have nothing more to say,
And there is no apparent reason ever for me to stay.
When all the fears of a lifetime
have crowded in on you
And every particle of your past
has lost all meaning,
When you cannot lift your head
or hold back the tears,
And you can no longer bear
the terror of your own ruminations,
When all your triumphs are as dust
that cannot hold you aloft,
And even the family you raised and loved
have no time for you,
I will be there
To bring you what joy and courage I can,
To remind you of all the beauty and wonder you
are,
To heal you with all the love I have,
To carry you, if need be, wherever you must go,
Only because you are my friend
And I will never desert you.

I Stand Like a Frightened Lamb

I stand like a frightened lamb
Amid the shadows of power
  That know where to go
  And how to get there,
  That demand love and attention
  And seem forever to receive it.
I wait for love, hoping it will come,
  Gently and unmistakably,
  Meant only for me,
Because someone takes the time
  To know who I am
  Without reading my astrological sign,
  Or hearing the highlights of my hero stories.
Once love came easily and I felt its warmth
  Wherever I walked.
Now it eludes me and leaves me whispering
  silently to no one
  On the stockpile of my own imaginings.
Does no one touch anymore without seduction?
Does no one love anymore without assurances?
I would give all that I have
  For one who loved me for the little I am,
  Who thought my face and eyes and history
    And my very being alone were deserving of
    affection.
Must I still play high school football to be worthy of
  love?
So I wake in the morning, fragile and afraid,
  And stand like a frightened lamb
Amid the shadows of power.

Fighting Everywhere in the World Tonight

Fighting everywhere in the world tonight,
   England crushing the Falklands
   Israel tearing to bits the PLO and Syrians
Like some ancient biblical battle one reads about
   And looks for the hand of God
      Or at least a fingernail.
Spokesmen on every side claiming righteousness and
   justice
      While heads are blown off, fathers and sons die,
      Brothers and sisters weep—and widows.
What does it matter if Jew or Gentile, Anglo or
   Argentine?
Meanwhile we stockpile our weapons and tear food
   from the mouths
      Of the aged and the poor,
Promising that no nation on earth will overtake or
   destroy us
      Save our own.
Once, as a boy, I could keep score of the Migs and
   Spitfires,
      The B-12s and subs and cargo ships.
Now I want to walk off the edge of the globe, take my
   chances in orbit,
Or disappear in a quiet forest where chattering
   squirrels
      Are content to stockpile acorns.
Mostly I long to be a boy again when it was only
   keeping score
      Of a distant football game
And mothers did not weep for their dead sons.

Where Has Time Gone?

Where has time gone?
Dick and I, best friends, wrestling on the
grass for three hours,
His flushed father cheering him on with
beer and wheezes,
My handsome, too proud father, laughing
and knowing I'd win.
Dick, sweating and stocky, strong as a
bull, I, small and quick and elusive.
Why did I not savor it all, knowing it
would be too soon gone, and unlike
later battles, would end
With hugs and cider and tollhouse
cookies?

Where has time gone?
Connie, with her blacks curls and peach
dimples, crushed by the crowd into
the back seat of a battered Chevy,
And permitting me to feel her softness
against young and startled thighs.
I, too decent and timid to lift her skirts,
but delighted to share the Little
Swamp where the blue racer lived,
And longing to lie with her staring
through the spruce trees at the lazy
summer sky.

Where has time gone?
    The bubbling, poet child to whom each
        day was adventure and each night a
        wondrous fantasy, and so much life
        to share.
    The peat mine and underground springs,
        the porcupine trails and the habits of
        bullfrogs,
    The climbing trees and jack-in-the-pulpits,
        the snake grass and nettles, the
        abandoned cabin and baby rabbits,
    The fragile forget-me-nots that wilted like
        forlorn lovers as soon as they were
        picked.

Where has time gone?
    I want to live life, every shred of it again
        and again,
    I want to live life, every decade over and
        over, forever.
    Every fight with Dick and every trembling
        pulse with Connie,
    Every sweat and hurt, every touch and
        sudden, unexplained tremor,
        The taste of sassafras, the tadpoles
            and turtles, a boy's every
            adventure again and again.

Where has time gone? My God, where has time
    gone?

Across the Rims of Distant Mountains

Across the rims of distant mountains,
Beyond the fog and shadows, the soft shades of
*   rose and purple,*
Where the disappearing sun lies concealed in
*   exotic wedding gown,*
I searched unceasingly in joy and sadness, fear and
*   wonder,*
Not sure what life meant, uncertain if I had seen all
*   there was to see, done all there was to do,*
Hoping I might finally feel the assuring warmth of
*   genuine love, believing that this alone could give*
*   beauty to all else.*
A gentle voice and waiting heart, shining eyes and a
*   soft smile*
Would tell me it was time to stop wandering without
*   direction and enjoy the laughter and wonder of*
*   the day.*
All that I ran from might be dissolved in love, all I
*   longed for could be found nowhere else.*
I have crossed many mountains and too many seas,
*   great rivers and oceans of deserts, always*
*   missing some integral part of me*
That I hoped finally to discover and connect in love.

*I bring memories and assorted fears, unuttered
dreams and untold secrets, but most of all
I bring a heart that seeks to learn what only
commitment can teach and nothing in heaven
or earth can take away.
I have wounded and been wounded, hurt and been
hurt deeply,
But never till now have I longed to be well loved,
never have I been so open to love from the
sheltered core of my heart and soul.*

*I have no way of knowing what future clouds and
daybreak brings,
I know not what sunlight or dark anxieties lie in
wait,
I only know that I want to remain at your side, to
explore life freely within the aura of our love,
That together we might uncover all the goodness and
joy, the happiness and peace that human love
can bring,
And that our love will encircle and enrich all those
we love and who love us as well.
I want to release and share all that I am, regretful
only that it took so long,
But profoundly grateful that I finally recognize that
the search begins and ends in love!*

When Love Means More, and Sunsets

As time passes
    And options disappear,
Love means more, and sunsets.
I want to stroll across green hills
    More than to climb mountains,
To laugh with children
    And hold their hands
More than to win wars and start revolutions.
Lately I listen more to the stars,
    Wise and utterly patient in their silent
        staring.
What is an hour or a year?
What is a week or a lifetime?
What is time
    When love means more, and sunsets?

When I Grey

When I grey, I want the young to laugh and ask
   questions,
   I want deer to nibble grass by the lake at
      twilight,
   And mallards to circle my pond cautiously at
      sunrise.
   I want to gaze at mountains I have climbed
   And dream of all the cities I have seen at
      midnight.
   I want to remember every love like a
      friendly landscape,
   And write the stories I had forgotten in life's
      haste,
   I want to sit with you in silence, share a
      thousand dreams without a word,
   I want to be friends with the whole world
      and a gentle guest of all the universe.

Most of all, when I grey,
   I want to be grateful for every breath,
   Forgiving of every least injury,
   Mindful of everyone I've hurt and thankful for
      everyone who ever loved me.

When I grey,
> *I want the days to blend softly into night,*
> *The darkness to surrender patiently to*
>> *dawn.*
> *I want to shout the history of my joys from*
>> *hilltops,*
> *And sing a new and passionate and never-*
>> *ending song.*
> *I want to laugh with lifeling friends at table,*
> *To exaggerate our triumphs drinking wine,*
> *I want to write as long as I am able,*
> *And thank the household gods that you are mine,*

When I grey.

Mainland China:
Shanghai: 1983

Land of laughter and lotus leaves, temples and
  pagodas, flowers and jewelled Buddhas,
Of a Great Wall challenging mountains and a great
  will forever hungry for freedom.
Land of deep, dark eyes and gift-wrapped babies, of
  warmth and innocence and eternal honor,
Of blood and revolution, poverty and energy,
  equality and liberation and a brave new hope.
Land of ancient music and gentle art, misty
  mountains and untapped power,
Of jade and commerce, pearls and wandering
  chickens,
Of autos and pedicabs, trucks and wooden wagons,
Of bombs and bicycles and palaces converted to
  parks,
Of computers threatening the abacus, and oxen
  reluctantly surrendering to satellites.

Land of Confucius and Marx, of tragedies and
  victories beyond all reckoning,
Oppressed by foreigners and its own traitorous sons
Betrayed by colonial greeds and alien creeds,

Too ancient to be frightened by time,
too wise to be circumscribed by passing theories.

China, I love you, your subtle sensualities and loyalty,
your profound spirituality and earthiness,
Your eyes and laughter, wrinkled elders and beautiful
children which tell me
That beyond custom and color and circumstance, I
am you, and you are me, brothers and sisters
forever!
China, beautiful, smiling, weeping, struggling, brave,
patiently liberated China, I love you!

All the Joy in the World

All the joy in the world takes possession of me today,
Unending nights and darkened days
forgotten,
Failures and unplanned frustrations,
rejections and angry confrontations
have lost their power.
Deserting friends I once missed,
Bitter enemies I once feared,
Promises never kept and dreams unrealized
Seem as nothing.
The sky belongs to me and the birds are assembled in
concert only for my ears,
Each towering tree, shaped by storms and time into
some impossible symmetry, is for my eyes alone.
The mountains, clear against the heavens, are my
personal delight,
The day is my private extravagance
And I alone can ravish and enjoy the night.
My own company satisfies, my own thoughts an
immeasurable treasure,
The breeze is music enough, bubbling streams drama
enough,
I make my own happiness and create my own climate
and weather.
I am a stranger nowhere, an alien no place on sea or
planet,
Forever at home in my world.
God is everywhere, love abounds, energy explodes
without prompting,
And I am grateful for every moment of my
life,
Grateful most of all to be completely, irrevocably
alive!

Grateful

Grateful tonight for the sight
    of a single star,
Grateful for memories
    salvaged from afar.
Grateful for this time of silent peace,
Grateful beyond all words
    when the mad echoes cease.
Grateful for deliverance
    from a private hell,
Grateful beyond
    what a human voice can tell.
Grateful for the wonder of human love,
Grateful for some strange guidance from
    above.
    Grateful for life,
    Grateful for rebirth,
    Grateful forever
    To live joyously on the earth.

INFORMATION ABOUT BOOKS AND TAPES AND APPEARANCES BY JAMES KAVANAUGH

The *Steven J. Nash Publishing Company* will supply you with all books and tapes of James Kavanaugh currently available. To receive information about James Kavanaugh's *new* books or tapes, lectures and workshops; to arrange appearances or TV and radio interviews; or for *The James Kavanaugh Newsletter*, write to:

STEVEN J. NASH PUBLISHING
P.O. Box 2115 • Highland Park, Illinois 60035
or Call: 1-800-843-8545

QUALITY PAPERBACK BOOKS OF JAMES KAVANAUGH
by STEVEN J. NASH:

There Are Men Too Gentle To Live Among Wolves *(57th Printing)* In this moving classic, Kavanaugh writes: "I am one of the searchers. There are, I believe, millions of us. We searchers are ambitious only for life itself, for everything beautiful it can provide...Most of all we want to love and to be loved, to live in a relationship that will not impede our wandering, nor prevent our search, nor lock us in prison walls..."

Will You Be My Friend? *(56th Printing)* Kavanaugh writes in this powerful, poetic reflection on true friendship: "Friendship is freedom, is flowing, is rare. It does not need stimulation, it stimulates itself. It trusts, understands, grows, explores, it smiles and weeps. It does not exhaust or cling, expect or demand. It is—and that is enough—and it dreams a lot!"

Laughing Down Lonely Canyons *(1986)* Kavanaugh brings his special blend of compassion, insight, and gentle humor to life's hard and hurting times...to those periods in our lives when we finally confront loneliness and fear..."This is a book for the barely brave like me, who refuse to abandon their dream...It is for those who want to make of life the joy it was meant to be, who refuse to give up no matter the pain..."

From Loneliness To Love *(1988)* At a time when the past freedoms grow dim, it seems hard to make intimate connections. There's a new kind of sexual warfare in which everyone loses the healing power of love. Kavanaugh writes: "To move from loneliness to love means to take a risk...to create the kind of personal environment and support we need. This is a book of hope and reassurance that love is available and loneliness can end."

Search: A Guide For Those Who Dare Ask of Life Everything Good and Beautiful. *(Prose, 1989)* "**Search** provides 12 proven principles to move from self doubt through self awareness to self love. It is a celebration of one's creativity and unique beauty, rising from practical psychology to the spiritual power of our Inner Being in a journey to wholeness." James Kavanaugh frequently offers an exciting workshop based on this book in various parts of the country.

Today I Wondered About Love *(formerly Will You Still Love Me)* This book was written in San Francisco and captured the soul of that city. Herein are some of Kavanaugh's most profound and gently humorous reflections on the man-woman experience. Burt Bacharach called this his "favorite Kavanaugh book."

Maybe If I Loved You More These passionate, lyrical poems confront forces that numb our senses and corrupt our values. Kavanaugh once again challenges us to be fully human, to move past private fears to simplicity and joy: "So much of life is spent trying to prove something...Maybe if I loved you more, I wouldn't have to prove anything!"

Sunshine Days and Foggy Nights This work contains Kavanaugh's most tender love poems, like the wondrous *Fragile Woman:* "too tender for sex, who will surely die—if tonight I do not love you." In words reminiscent of Joseph Campbell, he tells of the energy of any creative life: "The work I find most significant drains the least energy... my distractions are usually more creative than my resolutions."

Winter Has Lasted Too Long Kavanaugh sings of personal freedom and real love in a superb preface: "We shall be as free as we want, as mad as we are, as honest as we can. We shall accept no price for our integrity...This book is a heart's recognition that truth matters, love is attainable, and spring will begin tomorrow." Herein is the famed, "How much love I wasted on those I never loved."

Walk Easy On The Earth The book was inspired by three years Kavanaugh spent immersed in nature in a remote cabin in the California gold country. "I do not focus on the world's despair," he writes. "I am forever renewed by spring splashing over granite rocks, or a cautious deer emerging into twilight. I know then that I will survive all my personal fears and realize my finest dreams."

A Village Called Harmony—A Fable A powerful, eloquent prose tale that touches the deepest chords in the human struggle of lust and love, passion and peace. Dear Abby says: "It is a powerful tale of our times. A classic! I loved it!" The Detroit Free Press says: "Kavanaugh spins a sentence until it sings."

Celebrate the Sun: A Love Story A moving prose allegory about the life of Harry Langendorf Pelican, dedicated to "those who take time to celebrate the sun—and are grateful!" Alan Watts called it: "A stirring and unforgettable story that unites wondrously the wisdom of East and West."

The Crooked Angel James Kavanaugh's only children's story, newly illustrated in four colors, tells of two angels "with crooked little wings" who escape from isolation and sadness through friendship and laughter. A particular Christmas delight that sold out wherever it was displayed. Says Goldie Hawn: "My children loved it! So did I."

The Tears and Laughter Of A Man's Soul *(1990 Hardback)* "His most mature and personal ever!"—LA TIMES. With the power that has won "thousands of readers who never liked poetry before."—SAN FRAN. CHRONICLE. Kavanaugh touches our hearts, gently leading us from anxiety and near despair to love, laughter, courage and hope. He reveals a faith beyond dogmas, leading to the profound experience of "the Power within." He makes us laugh aloud and weeps with us in our struggle for freedom and peace. He writes as a man "whose theories have been tested in the laboratory of vast experience"—TAMPA TRIBUNE. The man who 20 years ago challenged religions and culture itself, emerges as a brave explorer whose struggles reflect the joy and hope of the human spirit. This is no book of poetic rhetoric, but "a saga of life and near death, scars and victory, falling and forever rising! It is the *tears and laughter of a man's soul!*"